Does Anal Retentive Have a Hyphen?

Todd Hunt, RARP
Recovering Anal Retentive Professional

Communication bleeps and blunders in business... and how to fix them

Does Anal Retentive Have a Hyphen?

Todd Hunt
Copyright ©MMXI

All rights reserved.
No part of this book may be used or reproduced in any manner whatsoever without written permission of the author and the publisher.

Printed in the United States of America.

Fourth edition 2011

ISBN: 978-0-9723692-0-6

"Does Anal Retentive Have a Hyphen?™" is a trademark of The Hunt Company and Todd Hunt, denoting a series of products that may include but is not limited to books, CDs and DVDs.

Published by:
The Hunt Company
2626 N. Lakeview Avenue
Chicago, IL 60614

Ordering Information

To order additional copies of this book, or to receive information about other products and speaking services, visit Todd Hunt online:

www.toddhuntspeaker.com

Also by Todd Hunt

Pardon Me, But That's a Really Stupid Sign!

"Communication Bleeps and Blunders in Business" Audio CD

"Todd's Take" Audio CD

"Communication Bleeps and Blunders in Business" Video DVD

"Crafting and Marketing your Killer Keynote" Speaker Learning System

Contents

Chapter		Page
	Introduction	xiii
1	He Doesn't Play!	1
2	The Key To Everything	5
3	No Theory	9
4	Client! Project! Situation!	11
5	Poultry Procedure	13
6	That's What You Ordered	17
7	Work At Last	19
8	Have It Our Way	21
9	How About Some Lemons?	23
10	Half and Half Again	25
11	Signs of Confusion	27
12	No Sign of Life	29
13	Lost In Translation	31
14	A-R Fun	33
15	Can You Top This?	35
16	Messing Back	37
17	But It's Not *Really* Free	39
18	The Joy of Paint	41
19	Super Size	43
20	Are You a P?	45

21	Phone Follies	51
22	It's On Us	53
23	Long in the Tooth	55
24	Secret Good News	59
25	Customer Disservice	61
26	Bar Code Bimbo	63
27	Online Oddity	65
28	Copy That	67
29	Dodgeball Fraud	69
30	Mute Point	71
31	Meeting Morons	73
32	Word Abuse	75
33	The Problem 8	77
34	No Problem!	81
35	*Too* A-R?	83
36	I Know	85
37	The "S" Disease	87
38	Cosmetically Different	89
39	Not For Nibblers	93
40	Inspiring Bosses	95
41	Just Give Me the Beep!	99
42	Useless Factoids	107
43	Parting Sign	109
	About Todd Hunt	111

Introduction

Extensive research reveals the five hottest topics in business today:

1. Sales
2. Customer Service
3. Leadership
4. Change
5. Poetry in the Workplace (OK, not)

When I started out as a speaker I thought I needed a separate speech for each of those topics. (Well, maybe not poetry in the workplace.)

And since I'm so anal retentive, I researched like crazy. Read every book I could find. Surfed the Web. Made color-coded file folders for each topic.

Then one day it hit me.

Sales, customer service, leadership, change (even poetry in the workplace)—all boil down to one thing:

Communication.

The biggest problem in business today. Because we all mess it up!

This book shows how to fix those blunders, and communicate better with customers and coworkers to become more successful.

1
He Doesn't Play!

I've been anal retentive for as long as I can remember.

In kindergarten, I did not play. I observed. Not because I was uncoordinated (OK, I *was* uncoordinated). It's just that the concept of play seemed so ... childlike.

Instead, I'd scamper out to the playground and observe kids. Fighting over the swings. Falling off the monkey bars. Throwing up on the merry-go-round. It was fun to watch.

And a chick magnet.

Girls would hang around me ... this five-year-old sensitive guy of the sixties ... I did not mind the attention!

But parent-teacher conferences were always the same. "Todd is an outstanding student and all the children like him. But he doesn't *play*."

My folks would come home and say, "You got a really good evaluation, but Mrs. Lawlor says you don't play."

Well, Dad, I'll tell ya—I prefer to leave play

to the kids who have nothing else going on in their lives.

I *am* anal retentive. I do not apologize; it's who I am.

You too, perhaps?

I suspect some people who read this book are also anal retentive (or "A-R," if that's a more polite term).

By the way, if you're not *sure* if you're A-R, then you're not (if you are, you know it well).

But never confuse anal retentive with organized!

If the money in your wallet is grouped by denomination (all the twenties, then the tens, the fives and the ones), you're organized.

If, within each denomination, your money is grouped by bill condition (crisp, then average, then ragged), you're anal retentive.

And if your bills are further sorted by serial number, this book won't help—because you have a much bigger problem.

Old-fashioned

You'd think that, being A-R, I'd be a total technogeek. Well, I'm not. Oh, I have a computer. With a built-in cup holder. Press the button, the little tray slides out, you put your coffee mug on it (mine broke off, unfortunately).

But I don't have a high-definition plasma screen TV.

And I don't have an iPod—I listen to tapes. (No, not 8-track! I'm not that hopeless. Cassettes.)

Nor do I own a Blackberry or smartphone. Just a cell phone that makes and receives calls. No apps, no texts, no tweets.

I'm OK. You're OK. Just be who you are!

Because if you're messed up inside, you're going to mess up communicating with other people. And we have enough of that already.

2
The Key To Everything

Communication.

We do it every day.

We start communicating the day we're born. And we don't stop until the day we get married.

My neighbor Bob says, "I've been married twice. Disaster both times.

"My first wife left me.

"My second one did not."

Love that Bob.

In case you're wondering, here's a little background on me (very little, because you're not wondering that much).

Born in Chicago. Grew up in Iowa.

A teeny-tiny town called Rockwell City. Population 2,316. When everyone's home for Christmas. If you count Janice Kretlow twice, because she's pregnant.

And everybody knows who the father is!

My grandma used to say, "This town is so small, the roadmap is actual size."

In Rockwell City, everyone knew everything about everybody. Communication was what we did.

During those formative years in Iowa, I learned a lot about communication. And I'd like to share some of it with you.

Textbook case

Step back with me to my high school. Rockwell City High. Student body 280, grades 9 through 12. Not a particularly broad curriculum ... but it did offer a journalism class. Sounded interesting, so I signed up.

For the first two weeks we read the textbook. On our own. We'd walk into class, sit down, open the book and read. At the end of two weeks, we had finished the book and were now ready to start writing stories for the school newspaper.

Except we didn't have a school newspaper. We had a school *page* ... in the town's weekly newspaper.

The Rockwell City Advocate. Came out every Thursday, whether there was news or not. So we'd all write our stories, turn them in and Carl would print them for us on our page.

Good old Carl. The newspaper's editor.

Publisher.

Reporter.

Typesetter.

Artist.

Ad rep.

Bookkeeper.

And consistent winner of Employee of the Month!

Yes, Carl would print our stories on our page. And that's what got me started reading the newspaper and developing a lifelong love affair with communication.

I'd grab the paper every Thursday and flip to our page first—to see how Carl mangled my great stories.

Then I'd thumb through the rest of the pages and get some chuckles out of the crazy headlines (this was long before a certain nighttime talk show host elevated headline blooper-spotting to high art).

We've all seen newspaper bloopers. Nutty headlines like:

Survivor of Siamese Twins Joins Parents.

Prostitutes Appeal to Pope.

Panda Mating Fails, Veterinarian Takes Over.

Two Sisters Reunited After 18 Years in Checkout Counter.

Man Struck by Lightning Faces Battery Charge.

Queen Mary Having Bottom Scraped.

I was hooked on communication. And that fascination stayed with me all through school and throughout my career ...

... as an advertising copywriter, direct marketing manager, ad agency director, marketing company owner, author and speaker.

3
No Theory

This book is not about theory. It's about real-life, lamebrained examples that make a point.

And there is no shortage of stupid in this world.

4
Client! Project! Situation!

I'd like to tell you about a boss I had at the ad agency Ogilvy & Mather.

Steve was very into "I am teacher. You are pupil."

I remember walking into his office one day and asking him about a situation I was dealing with.

Steve, we just got the merge-purge reports back and Donna is wondering if—he cut me off immediately, giving me a "time out" hand signal.

Then he pointed his index finger at me and barked, "Client!"

Zales Jewelers.

"Project!"

Fall credit promotion.

"Situation!"

The client is asking if we can reschedule ... etc.

I knew exactly what I was talking about, but Steve made me realize *he* was not mentally in that same place at that same moment. So I needed to set the stage and bring him up to speed before launching into my story.

And that illustrates our first communication mess-up.

Forgetting where our listener is coming from.

We have to consider that.

Because good communication is more than talking. And it's more than listening. It's *tuning in* to our listener and adjusting our communication style accordingly.

5
Poultry Procedure

You may be familiar with Boston Market Restaurant. But do you know the correct way to *order* there?

Yes, there is a right and a wrong way to order at Boston Market! I'm in the communication business. I study this stuff all the time. I have no life.

Let me tell you how *not* to order a meal at Boston Market. Do *not* walk in and say:

I'll have a quarter chicken, white, with mashed potatoes, no gravy, and cinnamon apples.

No sir!

In a perfect world, we *would* be able to place our order how ever we darn well please.

But that is not the *sequence* in which Boston Market associates (not employees, thankyouverymuch) process an order.

And since this is not a perfect world, they make us play by their rules. Which means *waiting*, and answering each question *as it is asked of you*.

"Welcome to Boston Market. My name is Rocko. I'm your poultry facilitator. Fritago?"

Quarter chicken, please.

"Fritago?"

Pardon me?

"FRITAGO!"

Oh—for *here*.

"What'll ya have?"

Quarter chicken.

"White or dark meat?"

White.

"What's your two sides?"

Don't say mashed potatoes no gravy ... because he'll say, "You want gravy on that?" Or he'll go ahead and give you gravy anyway.

Because when you say mashed potatoes, no gravy, Rocko hears only "gravy."

So say just "mashed potatoes."

"You want gravy on that?"

No!

Not "No gravy," because he'll hear only "gravy."

"What's your second side?"

Cinnamon apples.

Where is our listener *coming from*?

I know we're the customer and they should listen to where *we're* coming from.

But when they don't, we can either 1) suffer a complete mental meltdown; or 2) lighten up and answer *their* questions in the order in which *they* ask them.

Or 3) go next door to KFC. It's a lot easier.

Number 3, please.

"Original or Crispy?"

Original.

"Seventeen-minute wait for Original."

OK, Crispy.

"Day-and-a-half wait for Crispy."

OK, Tender Roast.

"July 29."

OK, good-bye.

6
That's What You Ordered

One night a friend and I went out for pizza.

Susan was in the mood for mushrooms, and I wanted sausage. So we ordered a medium pizza; half mushroom, half sausage.

Thirty minutes later our order arrived, but there were mushrooms *and* sausage covering the entire pie.

Excuse me, I said to our server.

"Ya??" she said (sounding a lot like Rocko's sister).

I don't think this is our pizza.

"Yes it is."

But we ordered half mushroom, half sausage.

"That's right. We only put on *half* the normal mushrooms and *half* the normal sausage."

I'm not making this up.

I learned that night how to order a pizza. I should have said, We'd like a medium pizza.

Now, Rockeena, imagine with me a circle,

14 inches in diameter. Let's draw a pretend line down the center of the circle, creating two equal halves.

I desire mushrooms, *just* mushrooms, on one half of the circle and sausage, *just* sausage, on the other half.

Oh—and would you cut it into eight slices, because we're not hungry enough to eat 12.

When you learn to lighten up, you deserve to have a little bit of fun.

7
Work At Last

My uncle Oscar, from Oklahoma, burst in while Aunt CeCe was watching television.

"Great news," he said. "I just found a perfect job. Thirty-five hours a week, three weeks paid vacation, full benefits ... and it's only 10 minutes from home!"

"That's wonderful, dear," she said, munching on a bonbon.

"I knew you'd be excited, honey. You start Monday."

Uncle Oscar and Aunt CeCe were coming from two very different places.

8
Have It Our Way

The line snaked out the door at my local Burger King. People kept coming back to the counter with orders that had been prepared incorrectly.

One weary woman handed her Whopper to the beleaguered coworker (not employee, thankyouverymuch). He summoned the manager.

Customer: I want just lettuce and pickles.

Manager: It comes with lettuce, mayonnaise, pickles and onions.

Customer: But I want just lettuce and pickles.

Manager: Lady, it comes with lettuce, mayonnaise, pickles and onions. What *don't* you want?

9
How About Some Lemons?

I prefer to eat my salad without dressing. Unfortunately, restaurants require you to wear clothes. [RIMSHOT]

I don't like salad dressing either. But many servers (not waitresses, thankyouvery much) find that hard to believe.

"What kind of dressing would you like on your salad?"

No dressing, thanks.

"No dressing?"

No.

"None at all?"

No.

"Not even on the side?"

No.

"How about some lemons?"

Fine.

Anything to make her happy.

10
Half and Half Again

Here's an interesting piece of research to keep in mind when we communicate with clients, employees, suppliers ... friends, family, spouses ... *anyone*.

We **hear** only half of what's said to us.

Understand only half of that.

Believe only half of that.

Remember only half of that!

That's why repetition is such an effective technique, especially when the same idea can be communicated in more than one way.

We used repetition in the ad business all the time.

All the time, we used repetition in the ad business.

In the ad business, all the time, we used repetition.

Where is our listener *coming from?*

11
Signs of Confusion

Another way we mess up communication is forgetting to *think*.

You know what I'm talking about. We see countless examples every day where people do not fully think through what they intend to convey.

Signs are a great source of *mis*communication.

I live in a high-rise. There's a sign on the door leading to the back entrance of my building:

This door must remain closed at *all times*

(What good is a door if you can never open it? That's not a door—it's a wall!)

How about these other sign blunders …

In the window of my neighborhood dry cleaner:

38 years on the same spot

In a Connecticut restaurant:

Open 7 days a week *and* weekends

In a Florida maternity ward:

No children allowed

In front of McDonald's:

Parking for drive-thru only

On a box of Nytol sleeping pills:

Warning: may cause drowsiness

Here's a brilliant one in the window of Ace Hardware:

Cashiers are not allowed to make change

(Then what good are they?)

I have 129 more, which is too many for this book. So I wrote a separate book called *Pardon Me, But That's a Really Stupid Sign*. You can order it online at:

www.toddhuntspeaker.com

12
No Sign of Life

Sometimes *lack* of a sign is just as uncommunicative.

I was in a Panera Bread shop. The drinks are self-serve. I put my cup under the Dr. Pepper spout, hit the button—nothing, no drink.

So I went back to the counter, found a Panera associate (there were no employees around, only associates) and said, Excuse me, did you know there's no Dr. Pepper?

"Yeah, dude—it's just a made-up name, like Aunt Jemima. She's not real either." (Rocko's cousin.)

Let me rephrase.

Did you know there's no dark, sugary, bubbly liquid emanating from the Dr. Pepper spigot?

"Dude—it's broke."

Brok*en*. Is the "Out of Order" sign also broken?

"Dude—they won't let us put up a sign."

So it's better to irritate customers than to

put up an ugly "Out of Order" sign scribbled on a napkin? Dude?!

The company probably mandates that "No sign shall deface the official decor of Panera Bread Shops."

Not even if it means communicating with customers, apparently.

13
Lost In Translation

The bigger the company, the bigger the goof. Especially in global markets.

In China, the name Coca-Cola was first written as "Kekoukela."

Unfortunately, nobody realized (until after they printed thousands of signs) that the phrase means "bite the wax tadpole" or "female horse stuffed with wax," depending on the dialect.

Also in Chinese, the Kentucky Fried Chicken slogan, "finger-lickin' good" came out as "eat your fingers off."

And chicken man Frank Perdue's slogan, "It takes a tough man to make a tender chicken," got terribly mangled in a Spanish translation.

A photo of Perdue with one of his birds appeared on billboards all across Mexico with a caption that explained, "It takes a hard man to make a chicken aroused."

I'll have the tilapia, thank you.

14
A-R Fun

Not everyone is cut out to be anal retentive (so many forms to complete). But if you *are* A-R, you can use it to mess with people who aren't.

I was in a Red Lobster restaurant, reading the menu. The server walked over and said:

"Do you have any questions?"

Yes. What's the capital of Ecuador?

"No, Mr. Smartypants! Questions about the menu."

Oh, the menu! Yes—what kind of paper is this printed on? Is the typeface Helvetica or Optima? Bold or extra black?

"I don't know—but I can find out."

How much is coffee?

"Dollar seventy-five."

How much are refills?

"Refills are free."

OK. I'll have a refill.

"Quito."

Pardon me?

"Capital of Ecuador. Quito."

Thank you.

"You're welcome."

15
Can You Top This?

Be careful what you ask for (remember "Where is our listener *coming from*").

A friend of mine walked into a yogurt store in St. Louis. She ordered a small vanilla yogurt, sprinkled with almonds.

How could that possibly be misunderstood? Small vanilla yogurt, sprinkled with almonds.

"You want sprinkles *and* almonds??"

Ah-ha! In St. Louis, sprinkles is a *topping*! Her mistake was trying to tell Rocko's brother how to *apply* the almonds.

He's a lactobacillus bulgaricus specialist. He knows how to get the almonds from the tray to the yogurt. So don't confuse the issue by asking for the almonds to be sprinkled.

Of course, if you *want* sprinkles—and you happen to be in Wisconsin—you'd better ask for jimmies ... because they don't know what sprinkles are.

And if you order "regular coffee" in Massachusetts, you'll get coffee with milk and sugar.

If you're dehydrated in New Hampshire, ask for a bubbler. Because they've never heard of a drinking fountain.

(They also call them bubblers in Wisconsin, but it's no big deal ... they don't drink much water up there anyway.)

16
Messing Back

Once in a great while you run across somebody who totally gets it.

Like my buddy Lenny at the Einstein Bros. Bagels near me.

I go in there all the time and order the same thing every time. Turkey and cheddar, toasted sesame bagel, plain.

Lenny knows that's what I want. So now he plays with me a little.

"Welcome to McDonald's! Whopper today?"

Yep.

"OK," as he makes my turkey and cheddar, toasted sesame bagel, plain.

"Want fries with that?"

Yep.

"OK!"

Super-size please.

"OK!"

Do you have the Superman action toy?

"We'll be getting those in next week."

OK.

It's *really* fun when there's a new person behind the counter, along with Lenny. He and I launch into our routine, and this poor girl tries to figure it out.

"Whopper? Super size? Superman? Lenny—we have Superman toys??"

"Yeah—they're free with every Happy Meal. Why don'tcha go down to the storeroom and bring some up!"

That's why I go to Einstein Bagels nearly every day. Lenny messes with me and I *love* it!

He knows when I'm coming from, I know where he's coming from. Communication.

17
But It's Not *Really* Free

I thought *I* was anal retentive … until I met the new director of advertising brought in by the major retailer for whom I worked years ago.

One of Judy's first tasks (after firing the deadbeat copywriters), was to purge the word "free" from our vocabulary.

"Buy one, get one free"—OUT!

"Free detergent with purchase of a washer"—OUT!

"Free eyeglass frames when you buy lenses"—OUT!

Why?

Because, she said, none of those things are really free. You have to buy something in order to get them. And free means you don't have to do *anything*.

I pulled out my dictionary, and sure enough:

Free. Not controlled by obligation.

So we had to change our copy to: "Buy one, get one at no extra charge."

Not as punchy as free, but truthful I guess.

It gets better.

I was working on an ad for the store's portrait studio. The headline was "Free 8x10 photo." I knew Judy would veto it, so I had my comeback ready.

"Todd, you know we can't say free."

But Judy, you don't have to buy anything to get the photo!

"Come on, they want you to buy extra prints, right?"

No doubt ... but if you walk in and want only one 8x10, they *will* give it to you for nothing.

"But you still have to do something to get it, so it's not free."

What do you have to do?

"Sit for the photographer."

The ad ran: "One 8x10 photo at no charge."

Does anal retentive have a hyphen?

18
The Joy of Paint

Judy's next order of business was to revamp our full-page newspaper ads.

Rather than "waste" space by showing myriad items (allowing people to discover something they might actually want), the new strategy was to feature just *one* item on the entire page ... and explain it in such exhaustive detail that everybody would rush out to buy it.

My first assignment: paint. A gallon of paint. I had to write 27 lines of copy, 40 characters per line, to fill the third of the page not taken up by the picture. Of the paint. The larger-than-life can of paint.

How much can you say about paint?

You can use it on a house.

You can use it on a barn.

You can use it on a fence.

You can turn things into different colors.
Purple.
Orange.
Puce.

You can brush it on.

Roll it on.

Spatter it on.

Throw a painting party.

Serve sandwiches.

Cookies.

Quiche.

But guess what Judy forgot?

If people don't want to buy, you can't stop them.

No matter how well you communicate.

(I won't mention the retailer. But it was named after its founder. And they shut down in 2000, after more than 100 years in business.)

19
Super Size

Whatever happened to small? Nowadays you can't buy a small anything.

Movie concessions are the worst.

I'd like a small Coke.

"Just medium and large."
OK, medium.

"Only a quarter more for large."
OK, large.

"Combo?"
What's that?

"Add popcorn."
Fine.

"What size?"
Small.

"Only super, king and colossal."
Make it a super.

"Only a dollar more for colossal."
Fine, colossal.

"Nineteen dollars, please."

Anybody remember nickel candy bars?

20
Are You a P?

A few years ago we received an office supply catalog at work.

Normally, this would not be an event of particularly epic proportions. We'd been ordering office supplies for years from another outfit and had no reason to change.

But I'm a marketing guy from way back, and the come-on in this catalog intrigued me. Right there on the cover: "99¢ special." Large box with all kinds of goodies spilling out of it ... pens, pads, paper, envelopes, file folders, tape and on and on.

It looked too good to be true. *All* that stuff for only 99¢??

Well, things were quiet that Wednesday afternoon at The Hunt Company (OK, they were dead). So I decided to call the 800 number and ask about it.

[RING]

Thank you for calling "Vestige," where every customer is a special customer. Your call is very important to us, and will be handled in the order in which it was received by the next available Customer Care Counselor. Thank you for holding.

[MUSIC ON HOLD]

Here at Vestige, we pride ourselves on the finest customer service in the industry. Thank you for holding.

[MORE MUSIC]

At Vestige, nothing will prevent us from giving you prompt, immediate attention. Thank you for holding.

[STILL MORE MUSIC]

"Thank you for calling Vestige, where every customer is a special customer. My name is Violet, your Customer Care Counselor. May I help you?"

Yes, I have a question about your 99¢ special.

"*What* special?"

The box of items for 99¢. It's on your catalog cover.

"Which catalog are *you* looking at?"

It says Sale Ends January 31.

"And *what's* the item?"

A box of office supplies for 99¢.

"Hmm—I don't see that on my catalog cover. Mine says 'Copier Paper Sale.'"

Mine does too, but that's on the bottom half of the cover. The top half shows a box with all kinds of stuff coming out of it, for 99¢.

"Hmm—I have no idea what that is ... unless you're a P. Are you a P?"

What's a P?

"Look above your name. Is there a code that starts with a P?"

Yes—P85642.

"That's it! You're a P. Sometimes they do special things for the Ps."

Well, it says ask for item number Y-11.

"Hang on a minute." She taps into the computer. "OK, here it is. 'Office in a Box, 99¢.'"

Great. Can you tell me what's in it?

"I have no idea."

Hmm ... I wonder if anyone else there would know.

"Hang on, let me ask somebody." She puts me on hold, comes back a little while later and says, "OK, I've got a copy of that

47

catalog now."

Great! Do you see the 99¢ special?

"Uh-huh."

The box with all the stuff coming out of it?

"Uh-huh."

Can you tell me what's *in* the box?

"Well ... looks like some pens and some pads and some ..."

I know that, but *how many* pens, for example?

"Oh probably one or two. Can't be *that* many for only 99¢!"

Can you tell me exactly how many of each item?

"I have no idea."

Can you find out?

"I have no idea."

Well, you get the idea.

Violet had no clue what her company was promoting in its own catalog!

At least to the Ps.

We all have customer service horror stories, don't we? About companies that just can't seem to communicate very well.

What about *your* company?

Do your sales reps, order takers, receptionists—everyone who deals with the public—fully understand what you sell?

Can they answer basic questions that customers and prospects might ask?

And do you empower your people to delight customers in every way imaginable?

Well, do you?

21
Phone Follies

We also receive the Hello Direct catalog.

We ordered an AT&T speakerphone. It worked fine for several months. Then one day it died.

So I picked up the phone (a different one, obviously) and called the AT&T support line. You can probably guess what happened next.

I was put on hold.

Transferred to 27 departments.

I *finally* talked to a real live human, who said:

"Send us the phone, we'll fix it and send it back within 14 business days."

I could not believe it.

Rocko had left Boston Market, and was now working at AT&T!

I don't know about you, but our business cannot stop for 14 days ... so I hung up and called Hello Direct, where we bought the phone in the first place.

I was immediately connected to Don.

I explained the situation and he said, "Mr. Hunt, we'll send you a new phone overnight tonight. You can send us back the bad one at your convenience."

At *my* convenience!

Not, "We can't do that."

Not, "That's not our policy."

The new phone arrived the next morning and our business barely missed a beat. I was *sooo* excited!

What do you think it cost Hello Direct to send us that new phone? A dollar ninety-seven. But what did it *do* for them? (I told *you* the story, didn't I?)

Hello Direct.

On the Web at hellodirect.com.

22
It's On Us

I'm not a technogeek. So when my computer zip drive died years ago, I called my trusty Zones catalog to order a new one.

It arrived the next day, but I could not plug it into my computer. So I called Zones and related the problem to Ron.

He diagnosed that I had ordered a USB connection instead of the SCSI required by my dinosaur computer. (What did I know?) They'd gladly exchange it for me.

"Let me give you our Airborne account number," he said.

Why do I need that?

"So you won't have to pay to send it back."

Let me understand—*you* are going to pay the return shipping for an item that *I* ordered incorrectly in the first place??

"Of course. We want you as a customer for life."

They've got me!

zones.com

23
Long in the Tooth

Unfortunately, good customer service is the exception rather than the rule.

I had my wisdom teeth removed rather late—mid 20s. OK, 30-something. Nearly 40, if you must know. Being A-R, I wanted to find out what to expect so I could plan accordingly.

But getting information out of my dentist was like pulling teeth. He shook his head and muttered something about wisdom teeth being no fun. Especially at my age.

I'm not looking for a thrill ride, Doc, just some information. Then I tried his assistant. "Wisdom teeth? You're sure not going to enjoy that!" I turned to the oral surgeon referred by my dentist, who proclaimed, "You are NOT going to have a good time."

Fine. I understand it's no fun. But what will it be? Will I be unable to eat for a day ... a week ... a month? Will I zonk out on the couch, unable to move? I turned the waiting room upside down, searching in vain for a pamphlet: "What to Expect When Your Wisdom Teeth are Removed."

There is no such pamphlet.

W-day arrived.

I went to the oral surgeon's office. He took an X-ray. Bad news. "Your wisdom teeth are fully impacted and lying on a nerve," he intoned. "I can't do it here—we'll need to reschedule for a surgical center." And that means what? "You don't want to know."

But I DO want to know! Will I miss work for a week ... a month ... a year? I talked with friends who'd had wisdom teeth removed, but none were lying on nerves, so I had no idea what to expect.

The surgical center called to confirm my appointment. Yes, I'll be there. "Remember to bring $1,000." OK, I'll have a check. "No, must be cash." What??

If they had explained this was my insurance deductible and they needed it up front, I'd have understood. But the demand for cash made me think they were running some illegal operation.

The surgery went fine. No picnic, but far from the unmentionable horror I'd been led to believe.

Here's my fantasy for a perfect customer service world ...

The dentist would say, "Todd, let me tell you what to expect when your wisdom teeth are removed. You'll be weak after surgery, so don't plan to drive home. Bring a friend with you or take a cab.

"You'll be too sore to chew for three or four days, so stock up on soft foods like popsicles, pudding and protein shakes.

"Since you're older, you may not bounce back as quickly as patients in their 20s. You'll sleep a lot, so take a few days off or work just half days for a week.

"You'll experience soreness rather than pain. Just take it easy."

Told you it was a fantasy.

24
Secret Good News

Have you ever dealt with a company that completely forgot to communicate *good* news?

I get the Chicago Tribune delivered at home Monday through Saturday. Not Sunday, because I like to buy my Sunday paper on Saturday at the grocery store.

One Sunday out of the blue a Tribune showed up at my front door. I didn't think too much of it—after all, there are more than 300 units in my high-rise. A mistake can happen.

Second week, another Sunday Tribune shows up. Well, maybe there's a substitute carrier who doesn't realize I'm only Monday through Saturday. It can happen.

Third week, another Sunday Tribune! Now I'm thinking I'd better call the Tribune and make sure I'm not being billed for this.

So I dialed the Customer Care number and spoke with a service associate.

Hello, I'm a Monday-through-Saturday subscriber, but for the last three weeks I've received a *Sunday* Tribune as well.

"I know," she said. "It's complimentary. We're doing that during the entire month of March for *all* our Monday-through-Saturday subscribers."

They couldn't *communicate* that to me??

It doesn't take a Ph.D. to slip in a bright yellow flyer that says, "Here's a Sunday Tribune with our compliments. Wouldn't it be nice to get one *every* Sunday? Now you can add it to your subscription at a discount price."

Don't keep your special deals a secret. Communicate!

25
Customer Disservice

As a recovering A-R, it used to really bother me when I'd get lousy customer service.

I'd bang my head against the wall and say, "*Why* do people do that?"

Now I just accept that some people wake up in the morning and are not happy until they make life miserable for somebody else.

Do you work with someone like that?

(Do you *live* with someone like that?)

I'm riding a bus in Chicago. An older woman gets on—obviously unfamiliar with the route—and says to the driver, "Do you stop at Burton?"

"Yep."

Very customer-friendly.

So she pays her fare, takes a seat near the front and stares intently out the window. She's looking ... looking ... waiting for Burton.

It's the middle of the day and there are not many people, so we don't stop at every stop.

The driver calls out streets.

"Armitage."

Ding! Somebody rings the bell, he stops, they get off.

"Menominee."

No bell, he keeps going.

"North Avenue."

Ding! Stops, people get off.

"Burton."

No bell, keeps going.

As he passes the stop, the woman says, "Was that Burton?"

"Yep."

"Well—I told you I wanted Burton."

And he says (I swear this is true):

"You asked if I *stopped* at Burton. You didn't say you *wanted* Burton."

I put down my New York Times crossword puzzle. And my Dixon Ticonderoga Number 2 soft lead pencil.

I sidled up to the bus driver, looked him squarely in the back of the head and said:

"I can't believe you beat out a million other sperm!"

He had no clue what I was talking about.

26
Bar Code Bimbo

I was in the grocery store. Buying my Sunday paper on Saturday.

The woman behind me put her items on the conveyor belt next to mine. So I picked up one of those plastic dividers and put it between our orders.

After the space cadet checker scanned my items, she picked up the divider.

Stared at it.

Turned it over.

Looking for the *bar code*.

"Do ya know how much this is?"

Actually, I've changed my mind. I don't think I'll buy that today.

"OK!"

I think she donated her brain to science before she was finished using it.

27
Online Oddity

A friend of mine saw a coworker putting a credit card into her computer and pulling it out very quickly.

When asked why, she said she was shopping on the Internet and they kept asking for a credit card number, so she was using the "ATM thingy."

If you gave her a penny for her thoughts, you'd get change.

28
Copy That

We once had an intern who was not the sharpest knife in the drawer. One day she was typing (on a typewriter—this was in the previous century) and turned to an assistant and said, "I'm almost out of typing paper. What should I do?"

"Just use copier machine paper."

So the intern took her last remaining blank piece of paper, put it on the copier and made five blank copies.

We can't let cerebrally challenged people get to us. It's their problem, not ours. And they're not going to change.

Sometimes we're thrust into stupid situations that *we* cannot change ... so we just have to deal with it!

I learned that in school when we had to play dodgeball.

29
Dodgeball Fraud

Did you play dodgeball in gym class, or was that an Iowa thing?

In case you're unfamiliar with this sport of kings ... you divide the kids into two teams (we all know who got picked last).

One group leaves their shirts on—the "shirts" team. The other takes their shirts off—the "skins" team.

I'm buff now ... but back then it was very traumatic!

Why did all kids play shirts and skins anyway? Who invented it? Was there ever a war fought that way?

The Shirt-Skin Battle of 1583 between the Huns and the Polyphoenecians has made it a tradition!

Anyway, you divide the gym in half: shirts on one side, skins on the other. The object is to *pulverize* as many kids as you can with an enormous rock-hard, red-ribbed rubber ball.

Once you get hit, you're out—and you sit on the sidelines for the rest of the game. The team that loses all its players first, loses. The other team wins.

And every kid learns valuable survival skills for life.

I still have nightmares about it. (I think that's what Hell is—an endless, flaming dodgeball game, and I'm a skin for eternity.)

Well, I'm the only kid in the history of the world who cheated at dodgeball.

How do you *cheat* at dodgeball? Easy.

When the coach is looking the other way, you *pretend* to get hit.

When his head swivels back and he sees you, snap your fingers and say, "Darn! I can't believe I got hit!"

Then walk off the floor with a really long face.

It was a stupid game!

I could not change it.

So I dealt with it.

There's a lot of stupid in this world. Which is good news if you're in sales, because people will buy *anything*.

30
Mute Point

Do you remember Marcel Marceau, the French pantomime artist?

Years ago he came out with a record—"Marcel Marceau Live."

A *mime*. With a record album (I'm not making this up).

What's next—a yodeler that uses sign language?

A ventriloquist with no lips?

This record was 44 minutes of silence. Followed by two minutes of applause.

And people *bought it!*

Not just French people—regular people like you and me!

I think that was the last Columbia House record on the list of 12 for a penny.

(Did you hear Marcel Marceau got arrested? The officer told him he had the right to remain silent.)

31
Meeting Morons

Why is it that otherwise sane, rational people suddenly catch a case of the stupids when they attend a conference?

Meeting planners go nuts at events, because of all the crazy questions they have to deal with.

"Which is cheaper, Early Bird or walk-in?"

"What time is the noon lunch?"

"Are the exhibits in the expo hall?"

"Is the general session for everybody?"

"Is the cash bar free?"

Don't ask those questions!

32
Word Abuse

I said earlier I grew up in small town Iowa.

I had a junior high English teacher named Miss Reiser. I think everybody had a Miss Reiser. She may have gone by a different name at your school, but underneath they were *all* Miss Reiser!

That A-R teacher who docked you if your capital Q actually looked like a Q, instead of a number 2, as on that green penmanship chart above the blackboard.

I once gave an oral report about geography, stating that Chicago has over two million people.

"Mr. Hunt! I hope you're in an airplane when you say that, because that's the only way you can be *over* two million people."

What Miss Reiser was saying is that "over" is a preposition ... and I should have reported, Chicago has *more than* two million people.

An annoying voice that woman had, but I never forgot what she said.

And that leads us to our next communication mess-up.

33
The Problem 8

Watch out for the "Problem Words."

There are eight words in English that give most people problems. We usually aren't even aware we're misusing them. But everybody does!

Over the years, friends, colleagues and, in one case, even a client very graciously (thank you!) and discreetly (thank you again!) pointed out my mistakes to me. And I never forgot what they said, either.

So here's a refresher course on Miss Reiser's eight words to watch out for. See how many *you* remember ...

1. Podium

Not the thing people stand behind while delivering a speech. That's a lectern.

A podium is the raised stage or platform on which a lectern sits.

And when we're at the airport and the announcer says, "Will passenger Anderson please step to the podium," she obviously never had Miss Reiser for English. If she had, she would say please step to the *counter*... or to the *desk*. Not the podium.

2. Hopefully

Means "in a hopeful manner."

In the movie *Oliver*, the little orphan boy requests more food when he asks hopefully, "Please sir—I want some more."

But we *hope* our new business pitch will go well.

3. Impact

The stock market does not impact investors. Middle East oil production does not impact gas prices.

I'm in my car, speeding along at 100 miles an hour and slam into a brick wall. *That's* an impact!

But the stock market *affects* investors. And Middle East oil production *affects* gas prices.

4. Data

I used to say, Here's what the latest data tells us. One day a client took me into the hall and said, "Todd, you're a smart guy, but data is plural—so you mean to say 'here's what the latest data *tell* us.'"

He was right, of course. By the way, just one is a datum.

Same with media. The media blows things out of proportion? No, the media *blow* things out of proportion. Because media is plural. Just one is a medium.

5. Over

Remember Miss Reiser: Chicago has *more than* (not over) two million people.

And LensCrafters does not make your glasses in under an hour. It's *less than* an hour. (Actually, it's not less than an hour—unless you have "standard" lenses and "standard" frames, which nobody has, so it's *more than* an hour.)

6. Myriad

Means many.

Your brother-in-law has myriad problems. Not *a* myriad *of* problems (you wouldn't say, "He has a many of problems;" you'd say, "He has many problems").

So the local mall has myriad stores. Not *a* myriad *of* stores.

And Las Vegas has myriad casinos. Not *a* myriad *of* casinos.

7. Irregardless

Is not a word.

Try looking it up—you won't find it in the dictionary. The word is simply "regardless."

8. Snuck

The past tense of sneak is *sneaked* (I know—it sounds wrong). Look it up.

So there we have our eight problem words.

Hopefully, Miss Reiser's data makes an impact—irregardless of the myriad of examples I've snuck into my talk, while standing at the podium!

34
No Problem!

Can we please eliminate "No problem!"

Would you tell me where the biography section is?

"No problem."

I need this shirt back by Tuesday.

"No problem."

Thanks a lot for your help.

"No problem."

Is it a problem to banish this expression from our vocabulary forever?

(And when did "you're welcome" become "no problem?")

35
Too A-R?

It happens all the time. People come up to me after my talk and say, "Todd, those eight problem words from Mrs. Reiser—isn't that *too* anal retentive?"

First, it's *Miss*, not Mrs.

Second, *too* anal retentive is redundant!

Does it really matter if we use the wrong word?

Does it matter if your doctor prescribes the wrong drug?

If your accountant uses the wrong tax table?

You BET it matters! And if you don't think it does, you need to meet my old boss from the ad agency Ogilvy & Mather.

Every time Steve received a proposal from a vendor or supplier with even *one* typo or misused word, he would toss it out of the running instantly.

"If they cannot communicate properly, I do not want to do business with them."

Another A-R guy with no life? Perhaps. But people *do* judge us by the words we use. So use the right one every time. You can't go wrong.

And we make Miss Reiser so proud, wherever she is!

36
I Know

Have you ever, you know, noticed how, you know, some people, you know, can't seem to, you know, say more than, you know, two words, you know, in a, you know, row, you know, without, you know, saying, you know, "you know?"

Ever notice that?

A colleague of mine sure did. So she came up with a way to correct it.

Every time someone says "you know," *you* interrupt and say, "I know."

I thought I'd you know ["I know"] stop by the store you know ["I know"] on my way home you know ["I know"] and pick up that stuff you know ["I know"] that we need, you know ["I know"].

It *can* be done.

You know.

(That like drives me crazy, like when somebody goes like, "Then he goes and then like I go" and like I just like want to like scream! You know?)

37
The "S" Disease

In spite of advances in medicine, there is a malady for which there seems to be no cure.

I call it the "S" disease.

It's easy to spot. Adding an "s" to the end of a word that should not have one.

I remember a presentation by a speaker who suffered from this affliction. Here are the three symptoms he exhibited:

1. **"Nordstroms"**

    The speaker raved about "the fabulous customer service at Nordstroms." Nordstroms does this, Nordstroms does that.

    But look at their shopping bag. Study their newspaper ads. Spell it with me: N-O-R-D-S-T-R-O-M. No "S!"

2. **"Krispy Kremes"**

    "How does Krispy Kremes differ from its competition?" he queried. "A Krispy Kremes is just a donut."

    Look at the sign on the building—the

last letter is "e;" not "s!"

3. "Days Inns"

The speaker shared a quote from the president of Days Inns.

The lodging chain is Days Inn. INN. One. No "s!"

This speaker was very knowledgeable in his field—clearly an intelligent, educated man. But his constant use of "s" where it didn't belong drove me absolutely nut!

38
Cosmetically Different

I ordered tickets to a play. They arrived in the mail, along with a little brochure outlining the theatre's privacy policy:

We try to call all our ticket buyers at least once a year to obtain feedback, update information and offer the opportunity to become more closely associated with the theatre.

Become more closely associated?

Could they mean contribute money? Are they just too chicken to say, "We're going to hit you up for a donation?"

We've become a society that doesn't say what we mean. For fear of offending someone, I guess.

That might explain why salesmen no longer exist, as in this radio commercial for a car dealership:

We don't have salesmen; we have product consultants.

That's a relief—I'd much rather be pressured by a consultant than by a salesman.

How about the money you pay for insurance? Not a premium, but "an investment in your future." So I have to hunt down a policy consultant in order to become more closely associated with the insurance company.

If you've been on a bus lately, you know that bus drivers have been replaced by bus operators. I don't know about you, but I want a driver, not a surgeon, in that seat up front.

Gambling is now gaming. Ugly is cosmetically different. Prisoners are clients of the correctional system. It's madness!

Subway Restaurant employees are sandwich artists. I'm sorry—slapping meat, cheese and mayo between two pieces of bread is not artistry. It's nothing to be ashamed of; it's just not Picasso.

Years ago, a company ran a radio ad with a gag suggesting that listening to three days of accordion music might be tiresome. You guessed it—they received a complaint from the Accordion Players Association!

Reminds me of the accordion player who drove home from a late-night gig. Feeling tired, he pulled into a local store for some coffee. While waiting to pay, he remembered he locked his car doors but left the accordion in plain view on the back seat.

He rushed out, only to discover he was too late. The back window of his car was smashed ... and somebody had already thrown in two more accordions!

39
Not For Nibblers

Look at a box of Triscuit crackers. In the upper right corner it says, "Not for Nibblers!" It's in their ads too.

That didn't make sense to me. Crackers are a snack food, right? You nibble on snack food, right? So why is Triscuit *not* for nibblers? Does it taste bad or something?

The more I thought about it, the more confused I became. So I called the Nabisco Help line: 1-800-NABISCO (622-4726) weekdays.

(I know—I have far too much free time.)

Would you believe—a real human answered? On the second ring!

Ray asked how he could help me today.

I don't understand "Not for Nibblers" on the Triscuit box.

"Well," he explained, "Triscuits are so good, that if you nibble you won't want to stop. That's why they're 'Not for Nibblers.' It's an advertising thing."

Oh—like the Lays Potato Chip slogan, "Betcha Can't Eat Just One®."

"Exactly!"

Maybe it's me, but I still think "Not for Nibblers" communicates, "This is a lousy snack food, so nibblers stay away."

(How'd you like that ® mark on the Lays slogan? Pretty A-R!)

40
Inspiring Bosses

Have you ever worked for a boss who truly inspired you?

I have—Harry. The boss who changed my life as an anal retentive.

Harry was VP of marketing at this insurance company. A solid, safe kind of organization for an A-R guy like me.

Harry was always fabulous.

People would see him in the hall and say, "Hey Harry, how ya doin'?"

"I'm fabulous!"

Either that or "Top notch!"

But mostly it was fabulous.

Harry was a laid-back guy, really nice and always fabulous.

There was a woman in our department who was even *more* A-R than I was. It annoyed her no end how Harry would conduct meetings without agendas ... make employees write their own evaluations ... never listen to his voice mail—that sort of thing.

"And how can he *always* be fabulous? That's statistically impossible!"

Harry and I were two of only three men in the entire department. And I guess he rubbed off on me, because I started to mimic his "fabulous" routine.

When people asked how I was I'd say, I'm fabulous! "Oh Todd, you're just as bad as Harry!"

Pretty soon I'd say it naturally, not only at work but to anyone, anywhere, who asked, "How ya doin' Todd?"

I'm fabulous!

It became a part of me. I didn't even realize it until years later, when I had my own marketing company, and was talking with a client. He said, "How are you today, Todd?"

Without thinking I answered, Pretty good.

"Oh? Just pretty good? You're not *fabulous??*"

Oh, sorry—spaced out. I'm *fabulous*!

My point is, nobody cares how you are. They really don't.

They don't care if you've got a boil. Or a

goiter. Or a scab the size of a Pringle.

That you keep picking at.

And it just gets bigger.

But you won't see a doctor—not after what your sister went through with that medical misfit, slimy snake-oil salesman.

They don't care!

So just say, "I'm fabulous!" Even if you're not.

You'll brighten their day.

You'll brighten yours too.

41
Just Give Me the Beep!

Now we come to my favorite communication mess-up.

Voice Mail.

When voice mail was new, nobody knew how to use it. Employees did not know how to program it. Callers did not know how to leave messages.

So companies large and small across this land had in-house seminars.

In fact, I saved a memo from my last job in corporate America. (Only a dyed-in-the-wool A-R would save a memo about voice mail class!) I proudly share it as a bit of history.

MEMO

TO ALL DEPARTMENTS

With the installation of the new company voice mail system, all employees will attend MANDATORY SEMINARS according to the schedule below.

Marketing: Thursday, March 26, 8:30 to 11:30 am.

Due to the nuances of voice mail technology, employees are required to remain in attendance for the entire three hours.

The seminar will include instructions on initializing your private voice mailbox, as well as a demonstration of the mandatory greeting format and menu features, including retrieving and archiving messages.

Employees will then practice personalized greetings and participate in voice mail role-plays for evaluation.

If you miss your scheduled seminar for whatever reason, a make-up session must be completed before voice mail can be activated on your phone.

Well, you know what? Voice mail's not new anymore. People *get it!*

Call your own work number, listen to your own voice mail greeting ... and say to yourself, "Self, can I be a better communicator?"

We've all heard voice mail greetings that sound something like this...

Hello, this is Dan McNitt of Allied Industries. Today is Monday, May 7.

I can't take your call right now because I'm either on the phone or away from my desk. But your call is very important to me, so please—at the sound of the tone, would you leave your name, telephone number, date and time that you called, a detailed (not a brief—no, no, no—but a detailed) message, when I can reach you, and I'll call you back just as soon as I can.

If you need immediate assistance, press 0 and

you'll be connected to our receptionist. Thanks for calling, and have a great day.

In case you've been living under a rock ... and have *no idea* what to do next ... the "voice mail lady" comes on, with *more* instructions.

To disconnect, press 1; to enter another extension, press 2; if you still want to leave a message for this person, press 3 or simply stay on the line. If you need assistance, press 0.

If you'd like to hear a duck quack, press 4. If you're calling from a rotary phone, get with the program!

Begin speaking after the tone. When you have finished recording, you may hang up—duh—or press star for more options.

Record at the tone. Recording. [BEEP]

I have now wasted 57 seconds—nearly a *minute*—waiting for the tone.

If I make 30 calls a day, that's a half-hour!

60 calls is a *full hour*!

Do the math ...

5 hours a week.

20 hours a month.

240 hours a year. Sitting. Waiting.

For [BEEP].

What about you? Do you lose callers in *your* voice mail maze??

A detailed message

I love that. "Please leave a *detailed* message."

So that's exactly what I do.

Hi Dan, it's Todd from the Hunt Company. 2626 North Lakeview Avenue, Suite 1312, Chicago, Illinois 60614-1811.

(773) 248-5790; fax (773) 248-5799; website: toddhuntspeaker.com

Today is Monday, May 7, 11:37 and 23 seconds, ante meridiem, Central Standard Time.

My favorite color is red ... I like my eggs scrambled ... I wear a size 10 shoe.

How much more detail would you *like*?

Kill clever

I know you are creative.

So paint a picture. Sculpt a bust. Write a poem about work.

But don't squander your creative genius on voice mail.

You know what I'm talking about. Clever greetings like:

That's right. You got the machine. We hate talking into these things too, but that's the only way we'll get your message. So leave yours after the beep.

Just give me the beep!

Hi, it's Bob. I'm out making my clients rich right now, so leave your name and number after the beep, and I'll call you back just as soon as I can. Wait for that beep now. Here it comes.

Just give me the beep!

Then there are the production numbers. Hollywood epics, complete with musical background.

[MUSIC: "OVER THE RAINBOW"]

Hello, this is Dorothy. I'm 'somewhere over the rainbow' now ... so leave your name and number after the beep, and I'll get back to you just as soon as I return from Oz!

JUST GIVE ME THE BEEP!

The best voice mail greeting I've ever heard is by a colleague in the ad business. I think it should be required operating procedure for every voice mail system on the market today. It's only six words:

This is Ann, leave a message. [BEEP]

My friends Lex and Janis have this message on their phone machine at home. It's only 10 words:

This is the Irvines, and you know what to do. [BEEP]

We do. We absolutely *do* know what to do, don't we!

But I have everybody beat, with this new message I put on my home machine. The world's *shortest* answering machine greeting...

Talk! [BEEP]

During the cold Chicago winter months, I often order food for delivery. When I call Marcello's, this is the greeting I hear:

Thank you for calling Marcello's. Press 0 to speak with an order taker.

I was hoping to speak with a team member or poultry facilitator ... but an order taker is fine, if that's my only choice.

And since order taker *is* the only choice, why can't one answer my call to begin with? I know, I know—all lines might be busy.

So the greeting could say:

Thank you for calling Marcello's. All order takers are busy, but your call will be handled next.

Don't make callers do extra work ... or force them to listen to your entire life story on voice mail. They just don't care!

Talking back

When we leave messages on other people's voice mail, let's be good communicators as well.

Give your own phone number at the beginning of your message and again at the end.

"Hi Gail, this is Todd Hunt, 773-248-5790. I wanted to fill you in on the client meeting we had this morning. So give me a call. 773-248-5790."

Why?

If Gail doesn't catch your phone number at the end, she won't have to listen to your entire message again. Just the first part, since you included your number at the beginning as well.

42
Useless Factoids

Sales, customer service, leadership, change, poetry in the workplace. Communication *is* intense, isn't it!

We've covered some heavy-duty intellectual material here.

But I want to assure you that, in spite of everything you've read in these pages, not *all* communication has to be profound.

Consider these interesting (but useless) factoids ...

- 33% of the population cannot snap their fingers.
- It is estimated that you will eat 40,000 cookies in your lifetime. (Already met that goal?)
- Americans spend twice as much each year for kids' athletic shoes as they do for kids' books.
- On average, an adult laughs 14 times a day; a child laughs 400.
- 67.9% of statistics are meaningless!
- 24 hours from now, you will have forgotten 80% of everything you

learned today.

So if you remember *just one thing* from this book, my hope is that you continually strive to improve the clarity and effectiveness of your communication.

Not like my cousin Herman, who walked into the drug store and asked:

"Have you got any of that prepared monoacetiacacidester of salieylicacid?"

Do you mean aspirin?

"Yes! I can never think of that word!"

43
Parting Sign

I'd like to leave you with one more sign ... and like everything else in this book, I'm not making it up.

It's an actual sign I saw in the window of a little convenience store, three and a half blocks from my house:

NO smoking. NO drinking.

NO loitering. NO browsing.

NO dogs. NO rollerblades.

NO shirt, NO shoes, NO service.

We appreciate your business!

And I appreciate your reading this book.

Keep on communicating!

About Todd Hunt

Consider a man who started a financial services company in Chicago, grew it to 400 employees in three years, then sold it and opened a bookstore in Vermont ... after appearing on NBC's "Seinfeld" for three seasons.

Todd Hunt did not do any of those things.

But he worked for a financial services company in Chicago, shopped at a bookstore in Vermont ... and watched "Seinfeld" on NBC.

Todd was in advertising for 10 years, at companies including Ogilvy & Mather, the world's largest direct marketing agency at the time.

For 10 more years, Todd ran his own marketing company in Chicago. Working with associations, retailers, nonprofits and financial groups, he sold insurance, seminars, theater tickets, memberships and other products and services to consumer and business audiences.

One day he discovered that people were eager to hear his funny, true stories about business. Now he speaks to hundreds of groups each year about how to communicate better with customers and coworkers to become more successful.

For a complete listing of Todd Hunt's books, CDs and DVDs, visit

www.toddhuntspeaker.com